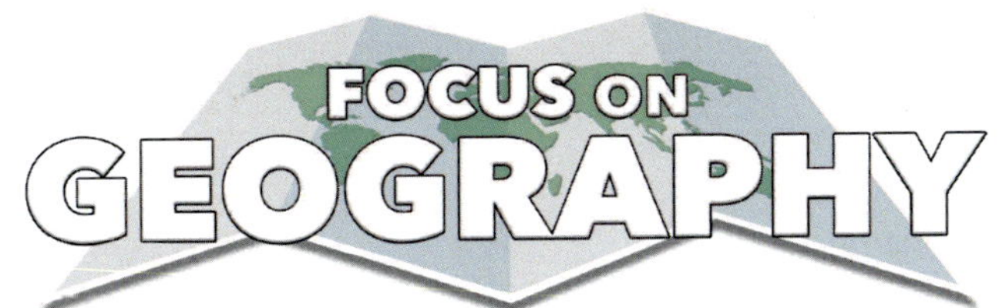

Focus on New Zealand

Natalie Hyde

A Crabtree Forest Book

Crabtree Publishing
crabtreebooks.com

Author: Natalie Hyde

Series research and development: Janine Deschenes

Editorial director: Kathy Middleton

Editor: Janine Deschenes

Proofreader: Melissa Boyce

Design: Tammy McGarr

IMAGE CREDITS

Shutterstock: Leonard Zhukovsky title page; Yevgen Belich TOC, p 36 (top left); Sheryl Watson, p 4 (bottom); riekephotos, p 5 (bottom left); Emagnetic, p 13 (middle left); cktravels, p 15 (bottom); Peter Gudella, p 15 (top right); gracethang2, p 15 (middle right); Emagnetic, p 17 (middle left); Arfi Binsted, p 18 (bottom left); travellight, p 20 (bottom); Norman Allchin, p 21 (bottom); Paolo Bona, p 25 (middle); Victor Maschek, p 25 (top); patrimonio designs ltd, p 25 (bottom); Emagnetic, p 27 (bottom); Lakeview Images, p 27 (top); Photos BrianScantlebury, p 32 (bottom); Alizada Studios, p 32 (top); Paolo Bona, p 34 (middle); lembi, p 34 (top); Laiotz, p 36 (top right); jixiang liu p 36 (bottom); rook76, p 37 (middle); Troy Wegman, p 37 (bottom); JoshuaDaniel, p 39 (bottom); RogerMechan, p 41 (bottom); Sheryl Watson, p 42 (middle); ChameleonsEye, front cover (top middle); p 18 (middle left); EQRoy, p 19 (top right backgroun); p 19 (top); p 20 (middle); p 33 (top left); p 34 (bottom); p 35 (bottom); p 36 (left); p 37 (top); p 38 (bottom); p 43 (top)

iStock: simonbradfield, p 6 (bottom); Gary Webber, p 45

Wikimedia Commons: Wildman NZ, p 8 (top); Schwede66, p 19 (bottom right); Public Domain_Matthew Grosso, p 24 (bottom); TheyLookLikeUs, p 30 (top); Eli Duke, p 33 (bottom)

All other images from Shutterstock

Crabtree Publishing

crabtreebooks.com **800-387-7650**
Copyright © 2025 Crabtree Publishing

In Canada: We acknowledge the financial support of the Government of Canada through the Canada Book Fund for our publishing activities.

Hardcover	978-1-0398-4294-6
Paperback	978-1-0398-4302-8
Ebook (pdf)	978-1-0398-4309-7
Epub	978-1-0398-4315-8

Published in Canada
Crabtree Publishing
616 Welland Avenue
St. Catharines, Ontario
L2M 5V6

Published in the United States
Crabtree Publishing
347 Fifth Avenue
Suite 1402-145
New York, New York, 10016

Library and Archives Canada Cataloguing in Publication
Available at Library and Archives Canada

Library of Congress Cataloging-in-Publication Data
Available at the Library of Congress

Printed in the USA/062024/CG20240201

Contents

INTRODUCTION 4

CHAPTER 1
The Land 8

CHAPTER 2
Becoming New Zealand 18

CHAPTER 3
Life Today 24

CHAPTER 4
A Vibrant Culture 30

CHAPTER 5
Looking to the Future 40

Glossary 46

Learning More 47

Index 48

About the Author 48

Introduction

A Day as a Mussel Farmer

It's 4 a.m. and the harvesting ship with a crew of six slowly makes its way out of a port on New Zealand's South Island. It is heading to the mussel farms at the Marlborough Sounds, a coastal area at the northern end of the island. Onboard, the ship has mini cranes that will help lift ropes covered in greenshell mussels out of the bay and onto the ship. The mussels have been growing for 18 months. A year and a half ago, farmers had moved the baby mussels, called spat, into the water. Finally, they are large enough to harvest. After the lines are pulled onto the harvest vessel, a machine strips the mussels from the rope. Next, they are cleaned, **processed**, and packed into bags. The ropes are taken back ashore to be washed and reused. By the end of the day, more than 110 tons (100 metric tons) of mussels are ready for market.

Around 212,000 people live in Wellington, New Zealand's capital.

New Zealand has more than 500 mussel farms. Most of them are in the Marlborough Sounds. The area's sheltered and clean waters are perfect for raising mussels and other seafood such as salmon.

Island Life

Mussels are grown in quiet bays all around New Zealand, an island country in the southwestern Pacific Ocean. A **remote** nation, its nearest neighbor is Australia, at more than 1,000 miles (1,600 km) away. The more than 5 million residents of New Zealand live on two main islands, called the North Island and the South Island, as well as several smaller islands. The capital city of Wellington is located on the southwest tip of the North Island. It is the world's southernmost capital city of an independent country. It grew from a Māori settlement and is now ranked one of the most livable cities in the world.

New Zealand's islands are known for their beautiful and varied landscapes.

The Indigenous people, or original inhabitants, of New Zealand are the Māori. They represent the second-largest **ethnic** group in the country.

The Country

New Zealand is ruled by a prime minister and is a **Commonwealth** country. The country is divided into 16 regions, each led by its own local government. The boundaries of the different regions largely follow natural drainage basins, or areas of land where water flows to a certain point, such as a river mouth or another body of water.

Several nearby islands are in a "free association" with New Zealand. This means New Zealand cannot pass laws for them, but can act on their behalf in foreign affairs and defense. These include the island nations of Niue and the Cook Islands. Another is the Ross Dependency, which is a part of Antarctica claimed by New Zealand. People born in these territories are considered to be New Zealanders.

Urban and Rural

Most of New Zealand's population, around 88 percent, lives in urban areas. In addition to Auckland and Wellington, major urban cities include Christchurch, on the South Island, and Hamilton, on the North Island. The smaller North Island, in fact, has almost three times the population of the South Island. In rural areas, farming is a significant part of life. From mountain glaciers to sandy beaches, New Zealand is varied in its landscape. Mountains make up around one-fifth of the North Island and two-thirds of the South Island. An island nation, it is surrounded by the Tasman Sea and the Pacific Ocean. At 9,300 miles (15,000 km), its coastline is the ninth longest in the world.

The New Zealand Scott Base research center is in the Ross Dependency. It is staffed by 200 researchers in the summer, and about 12 in the winter.

New Zealanders have a great respect for the natural world. One-third of the area of the country is protected national reserve.

Auckland, on the North Island, is New Zealand's largest city. Its population is more than 1.4 million.

Great Barrier Island
Auckland
Hamilton
Bay of Plenty
NORTH ISLAND
Tasman Sea
Cook Strait
Wellington
SOUTH ISLAND
South Pacific Ocean
Christchurch
Fouveaux Strait
Stewart Island

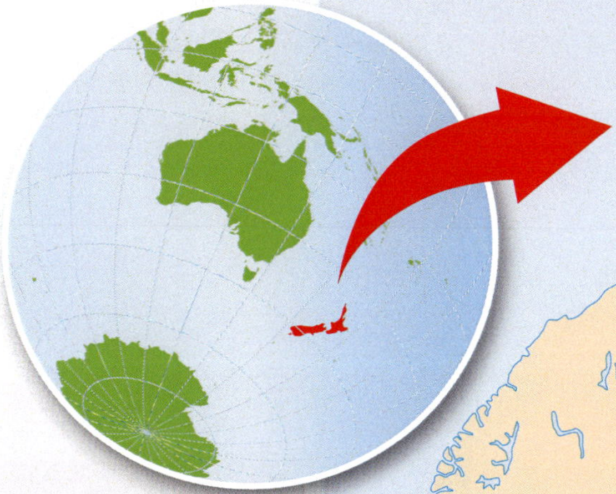

The Cook Strait is a waterway that runs between the North and South Islands. It also connects the Tasman Sea with the South Pacific Ocean.

AT A GLANCE

- **OFFICIAL NAME:** New Zealand or Aotearoa (Māori)
- **NATIONAL CAPITAL:** Wellington
- **POPULATION:** 5,128,000
- **OFFICIAL LANGUAGE:** English, Māori, and New Zealand Sign Language
- **LAND AREA:** 102,587 square miles (265,700 sq. km)

CHAPTER 1

The Land

Most of the land on Stewart Island is part of Rakiura National Park. Many native birds, such as the kiwi (above), are found there.

The land of New Zealand is very old. Some of the rocks date to over 500 million years ago! The islands of New Zealand are the exposed tops of a much larger landmass that is underwater. The country is made up of more than 600 islands. After the North and South Islands, Stewart Island is New Zealand's third largest. It is located 19 miles (30 km) south of the South Island. Just 400 people live there.

New Zealand is part of the "Ring of Fire," a horseshoe-shaped belt around the edge of the Pacific Ocean. The Ring of Fire surrounds multiple **tectonic plates** that shift against each other, causing many volcanoes and earthquakes. This is why New Zealand has hot springs and experiences earthquakes and volcanic eruptions. New Zealand has more than 50 volcanoes, some of which are still active today.

Rotorua, a city on the North Island, is known for its **geothermal** areas. It was first settled by the Māori, who cooked and bathed in the hot springs there.

Most of the world's earthquakes happen within the Ring of Fire. Earthquakes occur along **faults**. This fault can be seen in the mountains of the South Island.

To the Māori, Mount Cook is called Aoraki. It is within Aoraki Mount Cook National Park, a popular destination for climbers.

Mountains Run Through

Both the North and South Islands are divided by mountain ranges. The North Island's mountain range runs northeast through the center of the island. The mountains give way to **fertile** land, farmlands, and forested areas. Its coasts are covered in sand dunes. The South Island has larger mountains than the North Island, called the Southern Alps. They contain the highest peak, Mount Cook, at 12,316 feet (3,754 m). The Alps have more than 360 glaciers. These are huge rivers of ice that move down mountain slopes.

Closer Look

Island of Fire

New Zealand has 12 active volcanoes, with 13 significant eruptions in the last 1,800 years. The most recent eruption was the White Island, or Whakaari, volcano in 2019. Twenty-two people who were exploring the offshore island were killed, with many more injured. Tourism there was suspended following the eruption. Located 30 miles (48 km) from the North Island's east coast, White Island is still New Zealand's most active volcano.

Before the 2019 eruption, more than 10,000 tourists visited White Island each year.

The full Māori name for White Island is Te Puia o Whakaari, or "The Dramatic Volcano." It continually releases volcanic gas.

Water, Water Everywhere

As an island nation, New Zealand depends on marine resources such as oil, fish, and energy production from wind or water. New Zealand has special rights over the use of these resources in its territorial seas and its exclusive economic zone, or EEZ. An EEZ is an area of the ocean around a country, beyond its territorial seas. New Zealand has the fifth-largest EEZ in the world. It is 15 times the size of its landmass.

New Zealand's coastline has rugged cliffs, rocky shores, and sandy beaches. Beaches on the west coast of the North Island are black. This is because they are made of **ironsand**. There are also white sand beaches in the north. They are formed from **silica** sand, which is made up of almost pure quartz, a type of mineral. The coastline twists and turns along harbors, **estuaries**, fiords, **sounds**, and other human-made or natural landforms. These are sites for activities such as fishing and seafood farming, as well as unique environments for plants and animals.

Rarawa Beach, at the northern tip of the North Island, is known for its bright-white sand. The way the grains move against each other makes an unusual squeaking sound when walked on.

A fiord is a deep, narrow arm of the sea between high cliffs. Fiords are usually formed by glaciers.

Sutherland Falls, which drops 1,902 feet (580 m), brings tourists to Fiordland National Park on the South Island.

Marine Resources

More than half of the species in the surrounding oceans are native to New Zealand and not found anywhere else on Earth. There are more than 1,000 species of seaweed and 1,500 species of sponges. New Zealand waters are also home to almost half of the world's dolphins and whales. In shallow coastal areas, reefs house many sea-dwelling species such as snapping shrimp. Deeper ocean areas are home to varied marine life and rich fishing grounds.

New Zealand also has an abundance of freshwater resources. There are about 4,000 lakes and 70 major river systems that run for more than 264,000 miles (425,000 km). There are also glaciers, snow, wetlands, and springs. Historically, rivers were used to travel between villages. Today, freshwater resources are used for **hydroelectric** energy, household use, and **irrigation**. With rivers and streams flowing through the mountainous geography, there are many notable waterfalls that draw in tourists.

Shellfish is a traditional part of the Māori diet, known as *kaimoana* or "food from the sea." It is also common to use shells in home decorations.

New Zealand's largest natural lake is Lake Taupo. Like many of the lakes on the North Island, it formed in an ancient volcanic crater. On the South Island, many of the alpine lakes were carved out by glaciers.

Natural Resources

New Zealand is rich in natural resources. Fertile soil supports agriculture and forestry. Mineral belts provide many different mining opportunities. The long coastline and many waterways offer ocean and freshwater fishing.

The largest agricultural industry is cattle and sheep farming. Sheep are farmed for meat and wool, and cattle for milk and meat. New Zealand is the eighth-largest milk producer in the world. Most sheep farms are on the South Island because fine wool sheep adapted well to the climate. The North Island's fertile soil is perfect for growing stone fruit trees, such as peaches and cherries, and citrus trees. Grapes for wine are grown on both islands.

New Zealand has large **deposits** of coal, silver, iron **ore**, limestone, and gold. The most important mines are gold and silver. These metals are removed from hard rock using chemicals. Today, the use of these chemicals is managed so that toxic waste does not enter freely into the surrounding environment. Though mining is not a huge industry in New Zealand, it employs about 14,000 people.

Sheep farming is one of the most important agricultural industries in New Zealand.

Feijoas grow on small trees that were **imported** into New Zealand from South America in the 1920s. Today, the trees are thriving in New Zealand's climate.

The Māori use the wide leaves of Nikau palm trees for weaving. Other parts of the tree were also once used for home construction and eating utensils.

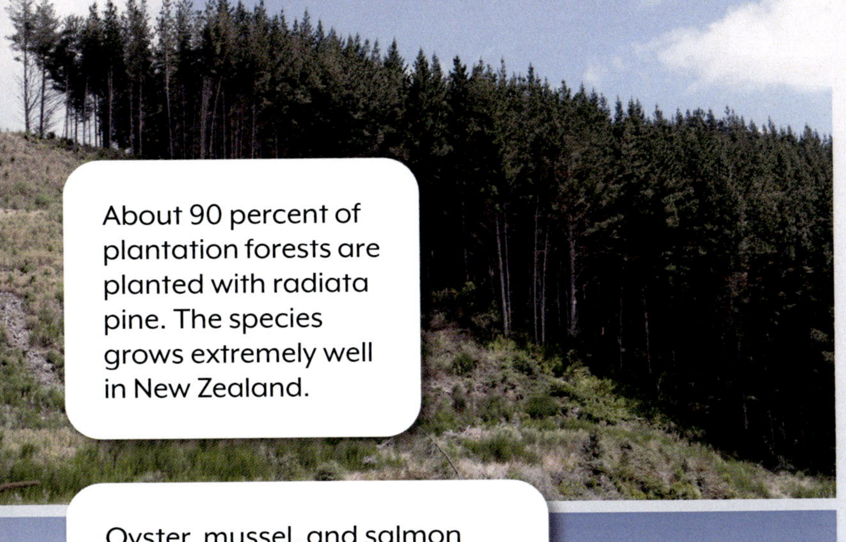

About 90 percent of plantation forests are planted with radiata pine. The species grows extremely well in New Zealand.

Oyster, mussel, and salmon farming (pictured here) are most common in New Zealand.

Forests have long been **revered** by the Māori for their beauty and spiritual value. They are known by many names, including *ngahere* and *wao*. Forests provide food, medicine, and materials for weaving and building. New Zealand has 24.7 million acres (10 million hectares) of forests. Today, 19.7 million acres (8 million hectares) are native forest, and 5 million acres (2 million hectares) are **plantation** forests. Plantations are **sustainably** managed and mostly planted with radiata pine, Douglas fir, and eucalyptus.

Marine resources play a big part in New Zealand's recreation, tourism, and fishing industry. The many lakes and rivers, as well as access to the ocean, mean there is a large demand for water sports and recreation such as kayaking, surfing, white water rafting, and diving. New Zealand has created an exclusive zone around all the islands for fishing. Fish farming generates millions of dollars in sales.

Settlements

Compared to many other countries, New Zealand has a low **population density**. On average, there are just 19.1 people per square mile (7.4 per sq. km). This is much lower than the United States at 94 per square mile (36 per sq. km), but more than Canada at 11 per square mile (4 per sq. km). Over 75 percent of New Zealanders live on the North Island. In fact, more people live in the city of Auckland on the North Island than all of the South Island.

The majority of New Zealanders live in urban areas. Many are in the four largest cities of Auckland, Christchurch, Wellington, and Hamilton. Three of those cities are on the North Island. Auckland offers good job opportunities with many industries and a large **commercial** center. Hamilton is the center of the Waikato farming region. Wellington is the political capital of New Zealand. Christchurch is on the South Island and is the second-largest industrial area in the country.

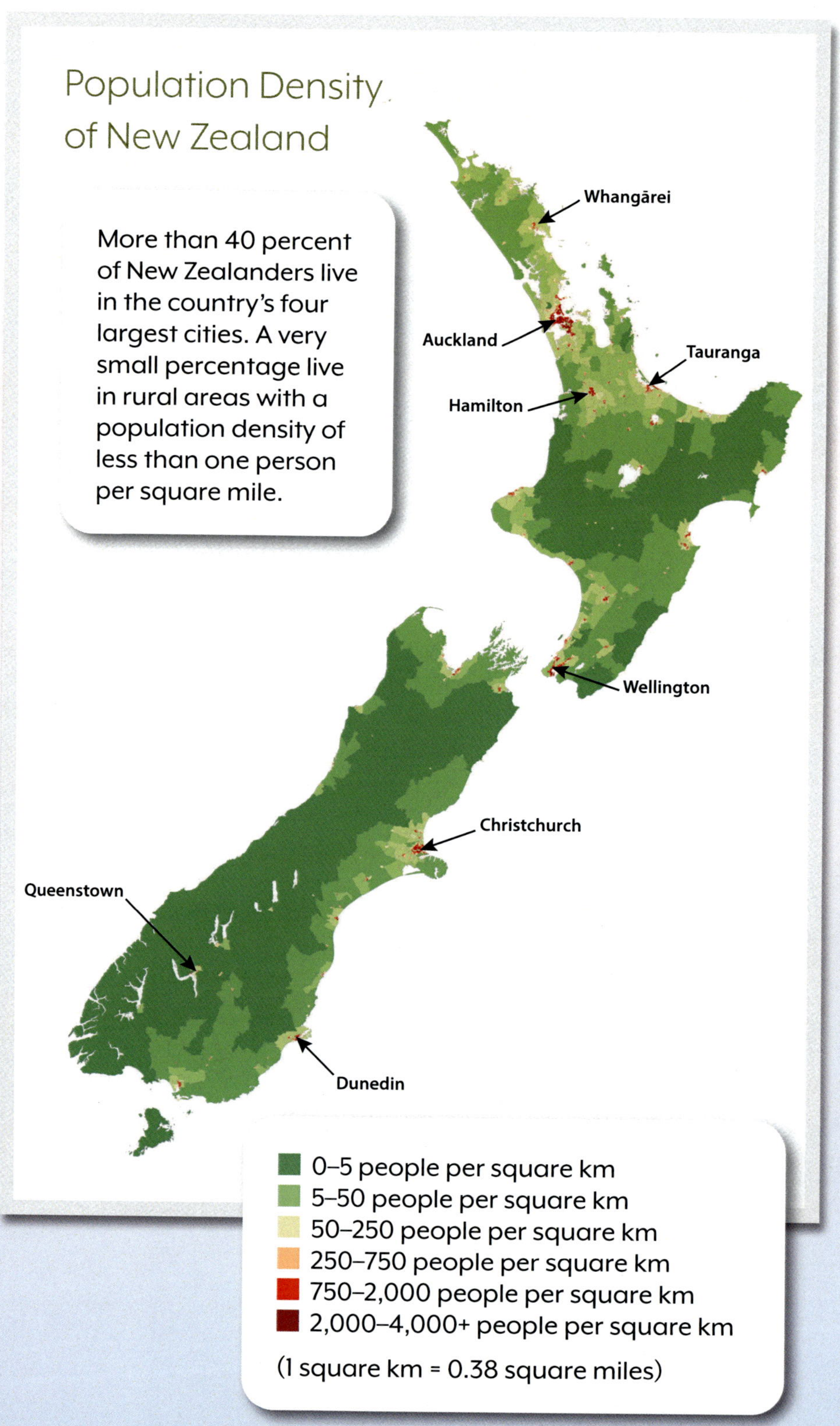

Even smaller towns in New Zealand tend to have airports, making the country more easily **accessible** for travelers.

Getting Around

Historically, New Zealand depended on waterways for the movement of people and shipping for trade. Main towns were near natural harbors. Today, New Zealand has a strong road and highway system. Because of the challenging landscape, the highway network depends on many bridges and other structures such as tunnels and sea walls. Ferries connect the main islands with nearby smaller islands.

The national railway is called KiwiRail. It began in the 1800s to transport goods to ports for **export**. In 1962, a rail ferry service was established so the trains could cross from one island to the other. Today, some railway branches into smaller communities have closed. The railway is used more for **freight** than passengers. Air travel has become more popular in New Zealand because it is easier to move around the mountainous country.

Water taxis are boats used to move people between islands where there are no bridges or ferries. Sometimes they are run like buses, with a fixed schedule. Other times, they are similar to taxis that take people wherever and whenever they want to go.

Aside from flying, taking a ferry is the only way to cross the Cook Strait between the North Island and the South Island.

Climate and Weather

New Zealand is in the southern hemisphere, which is the half of Earth south of the **equator**. Countries in the southern hemisphere experience seasons at the opposite time of year to countries in the northern hemisphere. In New Zealand, that means summer is from December to February, and winter is from June to August. In the north, New Zealand's climate is **subtropical**. It has humid summers and mild winters with higher rainfall. The south has a **temperate** climate, with cooler, more mild temperatures.

Surrounded by ocean waters, much of New Zealand has a **moderate**, maritime climate with mild temperatures, high rainfall, and a lot of sunshine. Summers are often sunny and warm, and winters are wet and windy. However, New Zealand's physical geography means its climate varies in different regions. The mountains that run north and south cause different weather from east to west across the country. The west side has more rainfall because warm, wet air rises up the mountains and releases its moisture as rain. The east side has warm, dry winds called foehn winds.

Snow is usually only found in the mountains in New Zealand, but there can be frost in the valleys.

The sunniest places in New Zealand are the Bay of Plenty (pictured), Hawke's Bay, and Marlborough.

Closer Look

Marine Heatwaves

Dark ocean waters absorb heat faster than lighter water, ice, snow, or land. A marine heatwave is a period of unusually high ocean temperatures. Recent marine heatwaves in New Zealand have been longer and more intense. Researchers believe this is caused by **global warming** and the La Niña weather pattern, in which strong winds blow warm waters on the surface of the Pacific Ocean away from South America and toward Indonesia. Warmer water carries less oxygen, which can damage or kill marine life. Marine heatwaves also supercharge ocean storms such as cyclones. Many of New Zealand's worst storms have been cyclones. Cyclone Gabrielle, in February 2023, displaced thousands of people, killed 11, and caused an estimated 8 billion U.S. dollars in damage.

Climate change is causing ice sheets around the world to melt and sea levels to rise. New Zealand's main cities will be at risk as most are on the coast.

Cyclone Gabrielle brought strong winds and heavy rain, causing severe flooding which damaged homes and **infrastructure**.

Native sponge species in New Zealand's coastal areas have experienced bleaching due to marine heatwaves.

CHAPTER 2

Becoming New Zealand

Polynesia is an area in the southern part of the Pacific with more than 1,000 islands, including New Zealand.

The Māori share their history through oral traditions. They trace their shared ancestors by reciting *whakapapa*, or their genealogies.

On the islands of New Zealand, the Māori cultivated *kumara*, or sweet potato, a crop they brought with them from Polynesia.

The first arrivals on the islands of what is now New Zealand came between 1250 and 1300 C.E. They were travelers from East Polynesia, now known as the Māori. The Māori migrated in large canoes called *waka*. According to traditional stories, the first explorer to discover New Zealand was a navigator named Kupe. It is said that when his wife, Kuramārōtini, first saw the North Island, she called it Ao-tea-roa, which means long white cloud. Aotearoa is still the name the Māori call the land.

The Māori settled and lived on the islands for hundreds of years before European explorers landed in 1642. They created settlements close to the sea or at river mouths, where they fished using nets woven from local plants and fishhooks carved from bone and stone. They also hunted seals and birds. The Māori grew vegetables they had brought with them from Polynesia, as well as native fruits and vegetables. They developed growing techniques such as warming the soil with fire embers.

Today, visitors can learn about New Zealand's history at the Waitangi Treaty Grounds, a historic site and the location where the Treaty of Waitangi was signed. The treaty is considered New Zealand's founding document.

Contact and Conflict

Early European explorers who visited New Zealand described the Māori as proud and fierce. The first Europeans to arrive were the Dutch in 1642. Englishman Captain James Cook arrived in 1769. Whale and seal hunters used New Zealand as safe harbors. By the 1830s, the British government decided to **colonize** the area.

In 1840, New Zealand's first British governor, William Hobson, took an agreement between the Māori and the British government all around the country. More than 500 local chiefs signed the document, called the Treaty of Waitangi. It made the Māori British subjects. In return, Britain would grant them property rights and tribal **independence**. However, these terms are under debate. Many Māori argue that the Māori-language version of the treaty, which was signed by the Māori chiefs, had a different meaning than the English version—especially when it came to their understanding of **sovereignty**.

In the years that followed, the British pressured the Māori to sell their land. Many Māori leaders felt that their sovereignty was being threatened. This resulted in a series of battles over more than 20 years, called the New Zealand Wars (1845–1872). In the end, around 3,000 people were killed. The majority were Māori. The British took over vast amounts of land. While some of this land was eventually returned, the damage to the Māori culture and society continues.

This bronze sculpture stands in Government Gardens, a public park in Rotorua, North Island. The two figures, one male and one female, represent the mixing of Māori and European cultures in Rotorua.

From Settlements to Cities

Auckland was originally a Māori settlement in 1350. It is on an **isthmus**, with fertile soil and two harbors. Its location also provided seafood and transportation. Those were the same qualities that attracted the British, who established the colonial settlement of Auckland and made it the capital of New Zealand. The capital was moved to Wellington in 1865, but Auckland continued to grow. By 1900, it was the largest city in New Zealand.

Māori legends say that Kupe, the navigator who discovered New Zealand, settled in the Wellington area. The Māori called the area Te Whanganui-a-Tara, or "the great harbor of Tara." In 1839, Europeans came to the area. They declared Wellington a city in 1840. It became the capital in 1865 because of its central location and harbor.

The first inhabitants of the area now known as Christchurch were hunters. It is estimated that they arrived around 1000 C.E. Māori tribes followed around 1500 to 1700, establishing settlements. A large settlement at Kaiapoi was a trading post for hunters and miners of pounamu, or a type of green stone. In 1839, Captain William Rhodes landed with a herd of 50 cattle. Soon, more farmers arrived, and a settlement was established. The Australian gold rushes also attracted more settlers to the area. The city was founded in 1856.

Auckland's growth was due to its coastal location and nearby industries, including logging, dairy farming, and manufacturing.

Wellington's harbor made it a center for imports and exports.

The large Māori population around Christchurch started to decline in the 1820s and 1830s. Conflict between tribes and diseases brought by European explorers were two reasons for the decline.

In recent years, the coal and timber industries around Greymouth have declined. Tourism jobs have replaced many coal mining jobs.

Greymouth is the largest city in the west coast region on the South Island. It was originally a government depot at the mouth of the Grey River. Areas around the river had first been settled by the Māori tribe Ngāi Tahu, who called it Māwhera. Once gold was discovered, the city of Greymouth grew and was declared a town in 1864. It later became a timber and coal center. It has both rail and roadways to bring in supplies and export mining products.

Many early Māori settlers occupied the southeast coast of the South Island. They built several *pā*, or fortified settlements. Europeans built a whaling station in Otago Harbour in Dunedin, a location that was originally the Ngāi Tahu village of Otakou. In 1852, the population exploded when gold was discovered in nearby Gabriel's Gully. Twenty years later, it had become New Zealand's largest city. Today, two universities bring many to the city.

Dunedin is the second-largest city on the South Island, after Christchurch.

Industry Development

By the late 19th and early 20th century, New Zealand's trade in furs, whale oil, and **flax** made it a country with one of the highest **standards of living**. Its main trading partner was Great Britain. When Britain's economy faced difficulties in the 1920s, it affected New Zealand as a result. Now, New Zealand's economy is strengthening as it develops new industries, such as winemaking, and grows its manufacturing.

The Māori developed the first mines in New Zealand. They **quarried** hard rock such as argillite, which was used to make tools. Europeans began mining in the 1860s with the discovery of gold in Otago, South Island. It spurred the first gold rush in New Zealand at Gabriel's Gully. In the 1880s, the Martha Mine was opened on the North Island in the town of Waihi. At the time, it was one of the greatest mines in the world. It is still being worked today.

Coal was first discovered on the South Island in the 1840s. The first coal mine opened near Dunedin, South Island, in 1849. Coal was found on the North Island in the 1860s. Now there are 15 productive coal mines. Coal is mostly used for power generation, especially on the South Island where no piped gas system exists.

Gold was found in the Arrow River in 1862. Chinese miners arrived to work, but were forced to live in huts on the banks of Bush Creek. Ruins of their community can still be seen today.

The Martha Mine produces around 1 million dollars of gold and silver every week.

Kauri tree

New Zealand's agriculture started by providing Great Britain with meat, butter, and wool. This industry is still an important part of the country's economy. Wool is still mostly exported to Europe, but the market for wool in China is growing. China is also New Zealand's biggest market for sheep meat.

Forestry was one of the earliest industries in the settlement of New Zealand. The long, straight hardwood from the kauri tree was ideal for shipbuilding. People also depended on wood from forestry to build homes, barns, fences, and railways. Sawmills were built and towns expanded around them.

Today, most of New Zealand's forestry is done on tree plantations. There, trees can be grown and harvested in a sustainable way.

CHAPTER 3 Life Today

New Zealanders are known for their laid-back lifestyle and friendly, but reserved, nature.

New Zealanders call themselves "Kiwis" after the kiwi bird that is native to the islands and a national symbol. The country is famous for its national rugby team, Māori culture, and beautiful landscape. New Zealanders are also known for their *manaakitanga*, the Māori word for **hospitality**. More than 90 percent of immigrants say that this welcoming spirit makes settling in the country easy.

The main cities in New Zealand are not overcrowded. With low population densities, cities offer many job opportunities. New Zealand also has excellent health care and one of the best public education systems in the world. It is, however, ranked 12th out of 79 countries for cost of living. It can be expensive to buy goods because as a remote island country, most items must be imported over long distances.

New Zealand's rugged **terrain** can make driving, public transportation, and delivering goods around the country challenging. Public transportation has a reputation for being slow and expensive. There can be delays when waiting for ferries to smaller islands, and air travel is expensive. Narrow and winding roads can make driving difficult and dangerous. Driving in the mountains is also risky due to snow, ice, and landslides.

At 85 letters, this New Zealand hill has the longest place name in the world. It roughly translates to "the place where Tamatea, the man with the big knees, who slid, climbed and swallowed mountains, known as the land-eater, played his flute to his loved one." Locals call it simply Taumata Hill.

Closer Look

Haka Dances

Haka are ceremonial Māori dances. They were traditionally performed when two tribes met each other, for a variety of reasons. Haka can display a tribe's strength, pride, and unity, or motivate warriors and intimidate enemies before a conflict. They are also performed at social functions such as weddings, funerals, and birthdays. Many people are familiar with haka as the pregame ritual of the men's All Blacks and the women's Black Ferns rugby teams. This haka dance is taken very seriously by the team players who display respect, passion, and **precision** in the movements.

Haka dancing often involves facial expressions such as bulging the eyes and sticking out the tongue.

The All Blacks perform the haka before each match. It is a way to show strength and power, intimidate opponents, and honor the cultural roots of New Zealand.

Haka is performed in a group known as a kapa haka.

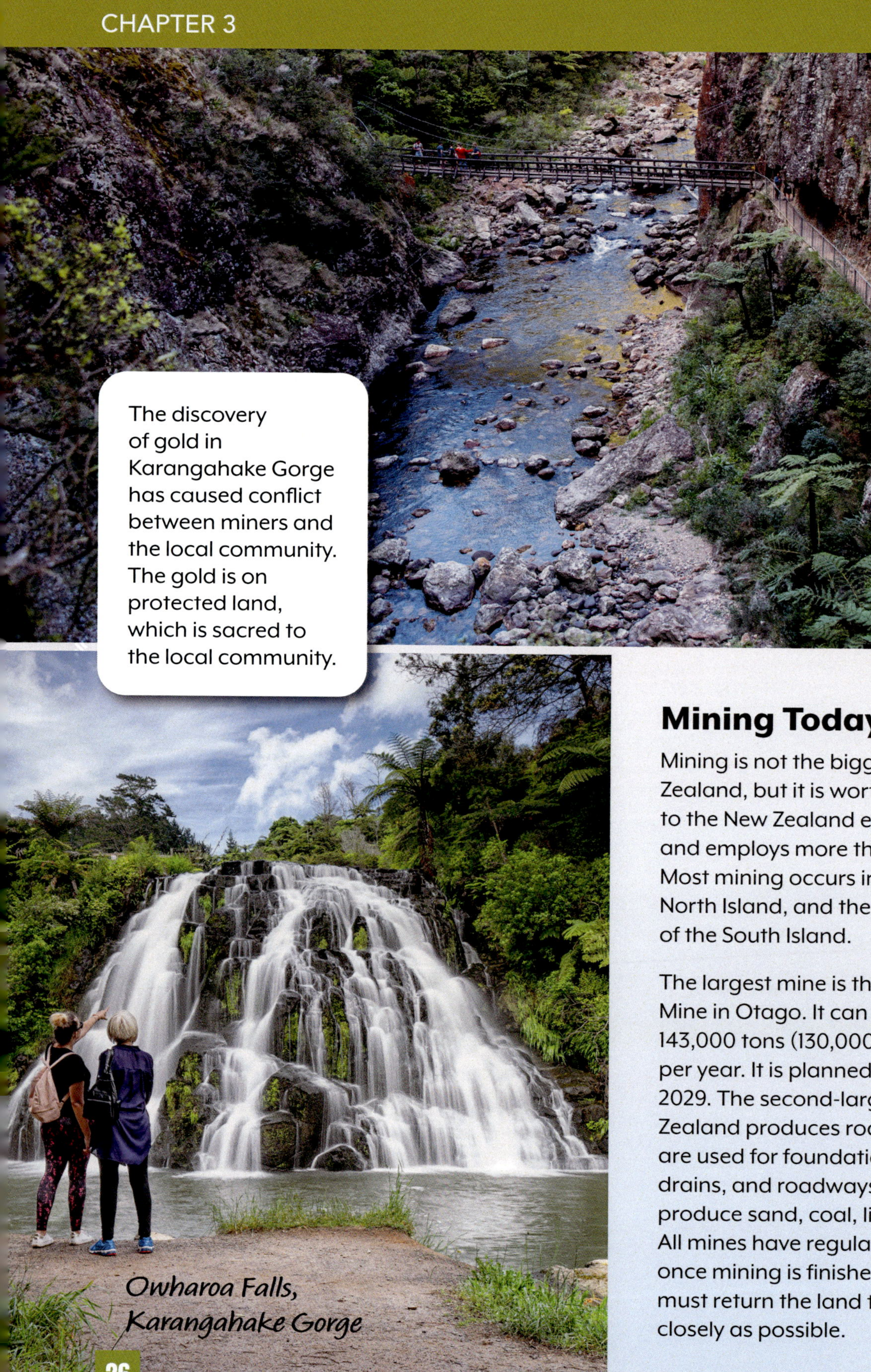

The discovery of gold in Karangahake Gorge has caused conflict between miners and the local community. The gold is on protected land, which is sacred to the local community.

Owharoa Falls, Karangahake Gorge

Mining Today

Mining is not the biggest industry in New Zealand, but it is worth millions of dollars to the New Zealand economy each year and employs more than 5,500 people. Most mining occurs in the north of the North Island, and the south and west coast of the South Island.

The largest mine is the Macraes Goldfield Mine in Otago. It can produce more than 143,000 tons (130,000 metric tons) of gold per year. It is planned to operate until 2029. The second-largest mine in New Zealand produces rock and gravel. These are used for foundations for buildings, drains, and roadways. Other large mines produce sand, coal, lime, and limestone. All mines have regulations that state that once mining is finished, mining operators must return the land to its original state as closely as possible.

New Zealand has coal reserves of more than 17.6 billion tons (16 billion metric tons). By the end of 2021, there were 15 operating coal mines. Most of New Zealand's coal is exported. Coal that is used within the country is mainly for generating power. New Zealand does not have much iron ore in rocks, but it has plenty in ironsands. Black ironsand is found on the beaches, especially on the west coast of the North Island. To get the iron from the sands, it is melted in electric furnaces until **molten** iron can be extracted. This is a process called smelting. The iron is then used to make steel.

The global demand for minerals used in clean technology, such as **rare earth elements**, has continued to grow. Solar panels, electric cars, and wind turbines all contain parts made with these minerals. New Zealand has the potential to supply many of these minerals. A search for rare earth elements has found more than 20 locations where these minerals might be found.

Most of the coal from Stockton Mine, on the South Island, is exported on ships to Japan, India, China, South Africa, and Brazil.

New Zealand is the only country that makes steel from ironsand.

More than 90 percent of the steel used in New Zealand is produced at Glenbrook Steel Mill, near Auckland.

Farming Today

Agriculture is New Zealand's biggest industry. Sheep and cattle farming are the most common, but deer, goat, horse, pig, and llama farming are also practiced on a smaller scale. As well as livestock, there are many fruit and vegetable farms. Oranges, lemons, and avocados grow well in the warm north. Nuts, olives, and berries thrive in the cooler south.

New Zealand's biggest export is dairy products. This includes products used to make infant formula in China, which is its biggest export nation. Most of the fruit grown in New Zealand is also exported, while much of the vegetable crop is sold within the country.

More than half of New Zealand's greenhouse gas emissions come from its agriculture industry. Much of those emissions are the result of the **methane** released as livestock digest their food. The government is beginning to tax farmers for the amount of greenhouse gas their industry produces. Scientists are also creating feed **additives** that reduce the methane that cows produce as they digest their food.

Most wine production is in Marlborough, where the soil is well suited for growing grapes.

New Zealand's wine industry contributes millions of dollars to the economy. Wine regions are on the east coasts of both the North and South Islands. The different soils and climate give wine from each region a distinctive taste. In 2016, the New Zealand government passed a bill—the Geographical Indications Registration Act—to allow certain regions to be registered as wine-producing areas. This helps winemakers promote and protect their product in a world market.

Deer were first brought to New Zealand from England. In the late 1960s, the deer farming industry in the country was established. Venison and **velvet** from deer farms are exported around the world.

Closer Look

Mānuka Honey

There are more than 700,000 beehives in New Zealand. Beekeepers produce an average of 24,250 tons (22,000 metric tons) of honey per year. Mānuka honey is made from bees that pollinate the mānuka tree, which is native to New Zealand. In addition to its delicious taste, the honey is known to have healing properties. It is used to treat wounds, soothe a sore throat, and improve oral health. Climate change, however, is one threat to mānuka honey production. Bees are threatened by habitat loss and rising temperatures.

Mānuka trees produce delicate flowers which are **pollinated** by bees. Mānuka honey can only be created in areas where there are many mānuka blossoms.

Vertical farms are springing up in New Zealand to fight the rising cost of living and provide a more eco-friendly way to grow food.

Sustainable beekeeping is being prioritized to keep bee populations healthy. This involves preventing diseases that affect bees and avoiding certain chemicals and **pesticides**.

CHAPTER 4 A Vibrant Culture

New Zealand is known for its stunning landscape, Māori culture, world-class sports, and unique wildlife. The great outdoors is valued by residents and visitors to the country. Any location in New Zealand is no farther than 80 miles (128 km) from the sea. Commercial bungee jumping began on Auckland's Greenhithe Bridge in 1986. New Zealand also has more golf courses per person than anywhere else in the world. The country has incredible natural beauty too. Blue Lake, for example, is the clearest lake in the world. It is found in Nelson Lakes National Park in the Southern Alps.

New Zealand is known not only for the animals it has, but also the ones it doesn't have. Sheep farming is so popular in the country that there are roughly five sheep per person. While sheep are abundant across the country, snakes are almost impossible to find. There are no native snakes in New Zealand. Some marine snakes, however, can be carried south toward New Zealand's northern coast. There is also only one native land mammal—the bat. Any other land mammals, such as rats, cats, wallabies, hedgehogs, and deer, were introduced by the Māori and Europeans.

Two species of bats are found in New Zealand: the long-tailed bat and the lesser short-tailed bat (right). To the Māori, bats are known as *pekapeka*.

Blue Lake's water is so clear that it is possible to see down almost 260 feet (80 m).

The steepest street in the world is Baldwin Street in Dunedin. At its maximum, it has a **gradient** of 35 percent.

Closer Look

Moeraki Boulders Beach

Along the north Otago coast on Koekohe Beach are strange round boulders. Each one weighs several tons and is up to 6.5 feet (2 m) in height. Scientists say they are made of mud, silt, and clay, held together by **calcite**, a type of mineral. Māori legends say they are baskets and **gourds** that washed ashore from a large, shipwrecked canoe carrying Māori ancestors.

Scientists say the boulders formed around 65 million years ago.

The unique beach is a popular photography location.

Unique New Zealand

Because the first settlers in New Zealand were the Māori, many of the country's traditions have their roots in Māori language, festivals, and food. The *hongi* is the traditional greeting of the Māori. It involves two people pressing their foreheads and noses together, representing the sharing of the breath of life. Another way to welcome guests is the traditional *pōwhiri* ceremony. Originally it was used to challenge guests to see if they came in peace. Today, it involves speeches, performances, and singing.

The hongi is still common when welcoming visitors to Māori grounds.

Hāngī is a traditional Māori way to cook food. The food is prepared underground in a pit oven. The food was traditionally wrapped in flax leaves, but today it is prepared in cloth, foil, or wire baskets. Then, the food is placed on top of hot stones inside the pit and covered with wet cloth and a mound of dirt. This method of cooking takes three or four hours.

Hāngī is a Māori word that means "earth oven." The method is often used to cook for celebrations because it allows a lot of food to be cooked at once.

ANZAC stands for Australian and New Zealand Army Corps. At this ANZAC Day event in the town of Mangonui, soldiers lay flowers at a war memorial statue.

The pōhutukawa tree flowers at Christmastime, during New Zealand's summer. The bright red flowers are perfect for decoration.

Celebrating Holidays

New Zealand celebrations include ANZAC Day, which remembers New Zealand's WWI soldiers, Queen Elizabeth II's birthday, on June 6th, and many food and music festivals. At Christmastime, many families spend their time at their bach. This is a word for a holiday home in a **scenic** place, often near a beach. At their baches, New Zealanders often use native pōhutukawa trees as Christmas trees.

Waitangi Day, on February 6th each year, is the national day of New Zealand. It is the anniversary of the signing of the Treaty of Waitangi between the ruling British and the Māori chiefs. Many consider this the founding document of the nation. It is a public holiday, and many Kiwis use it as an opportunity to experience Māori culture with concerts, film events, and performances.

The Hokitika Wildfoods Festival is the place to try wild food like this huhu grub. It also features foods such as mountain oysters, crocodile bites, duck heads, scorpions, fisheyes, pig ears, and worms.

Sports and Recreation

There are still many untouched and rugged places to explore in New Zealand. Hiking, camping, fishing, and bush and beach walks are favorite activities. With miles of coastline, it's no wonder water activities are so popular. It is estimated that around 40 percent of New Zealanders participate in boating each year.

New Zealanders are huge rugby fans, especially for their national All Blacks men's team. Rugby is the national sport of New Zealand. It is played between two teams of 15 players, each trying to get the ball into their opponent's in-goal area. Football, also known as soccer, is also very popular. It is played by more people than any other sport in the country. Futsal is a football-based game that is played on a hard court indoors. The BDO Lake Taupo Cycle Challenge is New Zealand's largest cycling event. Over 5,000 riders from across the world take part. There are different sections for cyclists of different levels. These include an e-bike event to make it an **inclusive** event.

Auckland is known as the "City of Sails" due to the many sailboats in its harbors and marinas.

The All Blacks are named for their black uniforms. The team has held the world rugby number-one ranking longer than all other teams combined.

Māori watercraft are called waka. Ranging in size, traditional waka were a useful means of migration and fishing. Today, waka ama is a sport that involves racing canoes. This sport celebrates Māori traditions.

Aoraki/Mount Cook is in the Southern Alps and is a **UNESCO World Heritage Site**. It is a popular tourist spot and a challenge for experienced mountain climbers.

New Zealand's stunning scenery is the backdrop for some amazing sporting events. The Queenstown International Marathon is an annual running festival. Called the World's Most Beautiful Marathon, the route runs between the Crown mountain range and the Remarkable mountain range. Another event is the Kathmandu Coast to Coast multisport event. Participants run, bike, hike, and kayak from the west coast of the South Island, across the Southern Alps, to end in Christchurch on the east coast. The Alps are also popular for mountaineering. The best climbing is from October to May, when there is mild summer weather and cool temperatures. The highest mountain in New Zealand is Aoraki/Mount Cook. At 12,316 feet (3,754 m), it requires experienced climbers. It takes six days to reach the summit, including glacier travel, crevasses, and ice climbing.

Sports and games have been an important part of Māori culture for generations. Martial arts, such as mau rākau, which teaches participants how to use traditional weapons, are practiced by people of all ages and genders.

Art in New Zealand

The earliest art in New Zealand consists of charcoal images found in limestone caves on the South Island. They are thought to be done by the first Māori settlers. Most of the images are of humans or mythical monsters. Other images include birds and fish.

Tā moko is a way to express identity and culture through tattoos. Different tā moko have different meanings. *Moko kauae* (right) are lip and chin tattoos received by women. They represent family and leadership. *Mataora* (left) are face tattoos traditionally received by men to represent nobility.

Master Māori carvers also make pendants out of greenstone, which is a stone found on the west coast of the South Island.

Māori wood carving, or *whakairo rakau*, is crafted from trees native to New Zealand, such as the kauri and totara trees.

Traditional Māori art consists of four forms: carving, tattooing, weaving, and painting. Māori carvings in wood, bone, or stone have special meanings. The *manaia* is a creature with a bird-like head and serpent-like body. Its image is used as a guardian against evil. Other patterns are based in nature, such as spider webs, fish scales, and ferns.

Māori tattooing, called *tā moko*, traditionally represented different Māori tribes or **ancestry**. Tattooists were revered and considered sacred. Māori weavers originally wove flax into baskets and fishing nets. Over time, these skills were used to create cloaks and mats.

These Māori women perform a traditional poi dance, where balls attached to flax strings are swung to music.

The architecture in New Zealand is mostly in a European style. The gold rush in and around Dunedin and Christchurch on the South Island produced the wealth for impressive buildings to be designed and built. Most buildings use local rocks and stones such as dark **basalt** and a lighter limestone.

Music in New Zealand has both Western and Polynesian influences. Māori instruments are called *taonga pūoro*. Most were flute or trumpet type instruments made from wood, stone, whale ivory, and human bones.

One of the most famous New Zealand artists was Colin McCahon. Born in Timaru, South Island, he was best known for bringing a new style of painting, called modernism, to New Zealand art. His landscape work depicted beaches, sea, sky, land, boats, and kauri trees. Emily Karaka is a New Zealand artist born in Auckland. Her paintings often depict the landscape, plants, animals, and mythic ancestors of her Māori heritage.

Colin McCahon's art is featured on this 1997 stamp.

All but one scene in *The Lord of the Rings* movies were filmed in New Zealand. Tourism related to the movies produces 33 million dollars each year.

Changes to Culture

There have been several waves of immigrants to settle in New Zealand. The first wave was the Māori from Polynesian islands in the South Pacific Ocean. The second wave was the Europeans who colonized the islands. The third wave was Asian and African immigrants, after immigration policies changed in the 1970s and 1980s. Each group influenced the culture of New Zealand.

Many Asians have arrived in New Zealand to live, work, and study. In recent years, many have been from China, Hong Kong, Korea, and Japan. More than 60 percent settled in the Auckland area, where they established communities in their new country. The Auckland Asian Association provides support to Asian communities and organizes social events that celebrate their culture. Most New Zealanders welcome immigrants. However, some have wrongly accused newcomers of threatening New Zealand's way of life, taking jobs, and increasing crime. Anti-Asian **racism** increased during the COVID-19 pandemic. To some Māori, increased immigration is seen as a threat to Māori culture and sovereignty, which was already damaged when the island was colonized.

The most recent census stated that more than 25 percent of Auckland residents identified with an Asian ethnicity.

These protesters gather at the New Zealand parliament building in 2017 in support of immigration.

Thai food is the most popular international food in New Zealand. Pad thai, tom yum soup, and curries are enjoyed in restaurants and cooked at home.

At the same time, tens of thousands of well-educated young New Zealanders leave each year, though this slowed during the COVID-19 pandemic. Reasons for leaving include feeling that there are more opportunities in other countries. This has resulted in New Zealand becoming more **multicultural**. One-quarter of its population has been born overseas. The government has programs to help immigrants connect with their communities, such as offering telephone interpreting services to help overcome language barriers.

In recent years, New Zealanders have rekindled their love of the outdoors and their focus on personal fitness. Activities such as hiking, camping, and working out have become more popular. The food scene is also growing. International foods have been increasing in popularity. There is also a growing movement to bring the traditions of Māori food forward. Indigenous ingredients and cooking methods are being introduced in fine dining restaurants, pop-up eateries, and bistros.

New Zealanders celebrate Hindu culture at the Holi Festival in Wellington.

CHAPTER 5

Looking to the Future

Climate change is affecting New Zealand's vineyards. Warmer temperatures mean grapevines flower earlier, affecting harvesting schedules and the quality of the wine. Growers are trying to adapt by growing varieties that tolerate the heat better, or flower and ripen later.

Like many countries around the world, the future of New Zealand has both possibilities and challenges. The environment plays such a crucial role in the health of the land, animals, plants, and people that its needs are of top importance.

Native plants and animals are under threat from other species that have been brought into the country. The government plans to get rid of all possums, rats, and stoats by 2050. Possums feed on new shoots and flowers, preventing plants from growing and spreading. Stoats, which are members of the weasel family, prey on birds' eggs, chicks, and even nesting adults. Stoats have played a part in the disappearance of the bush wren and laughing owl.

Farming and forestry practices are contributing to pollution and climate change. Recent studies estimate that 45 percent of New Zealand's rivers are not safe for swimming. Chemicals, fertilizers, and **nitrogen** from dairy cattle run off the fields and into waterways. Urban areas are also polluted. Air pollution is often the result of coal burning for home heating.

A recent government study of freshwater ecosystems in New Zealand identified that many native species of fish and birds are threatened with extinction.

"Pine"troleum may replace oil in the future. A New Zealand company called Futurily is developing technology that uses pine trees, instead of oil, in products such as paints and concrete.

New Zealand is behind the rest of the world when it comes to clean technology. Because it is a remote island country dependent on its farming industry, there are fewer factors pushing it to change. However, there are some successes. About 80 percent of New Zealand's electricity comes from renewable resources.

There are programs to put solar panels on dairy sheds across the country. There are also several companies using geothermal energy to cool and heat homes. The government is taking measures to help new green companies get started. It has also committed to reducing greenhouse gases by 30 percent by 2030.

The Wairakei Power Station on the North Island uses geothermal energy to create power. Geothermal energy comes from heat under Earth's surface. New Zealand, with its volcanic activity, is a country with a lot of access to geothermal energy.

The Future of New Zealand's Industries

Industry Transformation Plans are being used to change the major industries in New Zealand. ITPs are created in partnerships with businesses, workers, the Māori, and the government. These plans set long-term goals for each industry to create higher wages, high **productivity**, and less harm to the environment.

The large EEZ in New Zealand's surrounding oceans is not only a source of fish and **aquaculture**, but it also has mining potential. New Zealand is considering mining for deep-sea mineral deposits near seafloor hot springs. Hot springs are spots on the seafloor where there are cracks in Earth's crust. There, water heated deep inside the Earth flows out. When this hot water meets the cold seawater, metals and minerals such as gold, copper, lead, zinc, and iron clump together in lumps called nodules. Mining companies can then extract these metals. It is considered a renewable resource because these mineral nodules are constantly being formed.

One area of focus within New Zealand's Industry Transformation Plans is agritech. This is the use of technology to innovate agricultural practices, making them more profitable and sustainable.

There is opposition to seabed mining by environmental groups, who point to the potential damage that could be done to the ocean floor.

A Fisheries Industry Transformation Plan aims to support people who work in the industry or live in nearby communities, with new jobs and **nutritional** seafood.

New Zealand's tourism is focused on sustainable travel. Sustainable travel includes energy efficiency, waste management, recycling, minimizing water usage, and supporting the local community.

Manufacturing and retail industries must compete with countries that have lower production costs. To deal with this, New Zealand companies are trying to focus on smaller, more specialized markets. These include new varieties of wine, exotic fruits, ostrich feathers, carpet weaving, and yacht construction. Agriculture also faces challenges as people around the world turn to alternative sources of protein other than animal meat. This may threaten New Zealand's farm economy.

Tourism contributes billions of dollars to New Zealand's economy. There is concern that if international air travel continues to go up in price, New Zealand will be considered too far away from many tourists to be affordable. New Zealand has also created a "tourist tax." The International Visitor Levy (IVL) is a one-time payment of 35 New Zealand dollars. The government plans to use the estimated 450 million dollars it earns to combat invasive animal species and fight habitat loss.

Future Changes and Challenges

New Zealand is facing a series of major shifts that will have a lasting impact on its society. These include where people are settling, the economy, immigration, and the environment. New Zealand is one of the world's most **susceptible** countries to a rise in natural disasters due to climate change. This is because of its location and geography. Surrounded by ocean, warming water will contribute to more frequent extreme weather such as changing rainfall, droughts, and fire risk. New Zealand's location on the Pacific "Ring of Fire" also results in earthquakes and volcanic activity.

Extreme weather is becoming more common due to climate change. Droughts can significantly impact agriculture, an essential industry in New Zealand.

With sea levels rising due to global warming, coastal erosion and flooding is a concern in New Zealand. Two-thirds of New Zealanders live within 3 miles (5 km) of the coast. Some solutions could include building homes farther from the coast and adding seawalls along the coast.

The government is looking at policies to close the wage gap among different worker groups. Fair Pay Agreements are a new part of New Zealand's employment laws. These agreements work to create minimum standards for certain jobs such as security, hospitality, and cleaning. They cover things like pay, working hours, time off, and health and safety.

Like many countries, New Zealand has an aging population. Kiwis over 65 years old will outnumber those under 15 years old by 2025. An older population can put a strain on health services and the need for accessible homes and businesses. Laws will need to be passed to protect the rights and interests of older citizens. This could involve establishing services that help them live longer at home and continue to make decisions for themselves.

The New Zealand government is committed to reaching a net-zero emission rate by 2050. Net-zero emissions means that a region or country balances the amount of greenhouse gases it releases into the atmosphere with the amount it takes out. Greenhouse gases are gases, such as carbon dioxide, that trap heat in Earth's atmosphere. They can be taken out of the atmosphere by switching away from using fossil fuels or planting new forests. Trees take in carbon dioxide as they grow. By reaching net-zero emissions, New Zealand can help provide its ecotourism and products with a clean, green image.

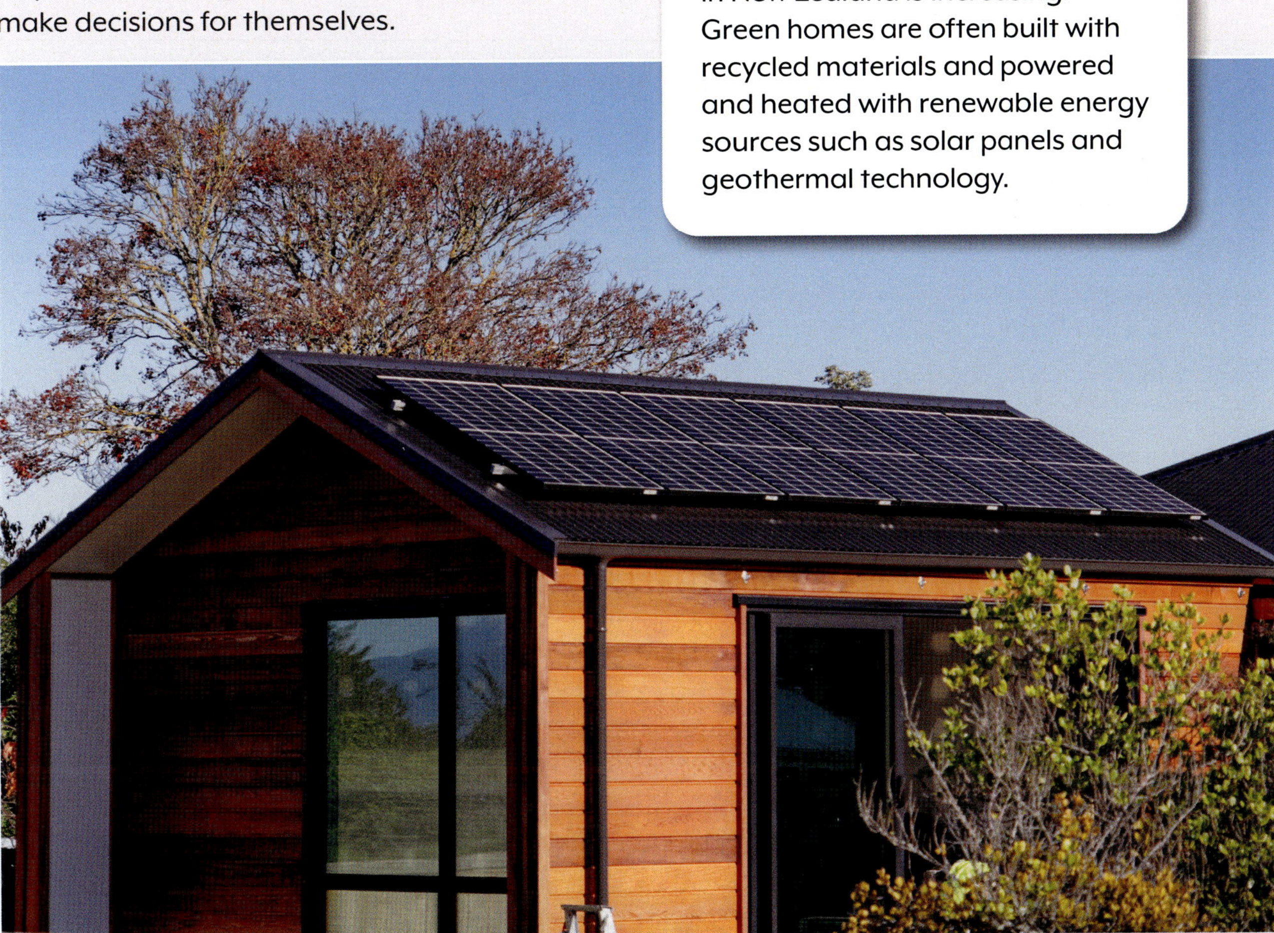

The number of green homes in New Zealand is increasing. Green homes are often built with recycled materials and powered and heated with renewable energy sources such as solar panels and geothermal technology.

accessible Easily reached

additives Substances added to something

ancestry Family history

aquaculture Farming of fish and seafood in water environments

basalt A dark rock produced by volcanoes

calcite A white or clear mineral made up of calcium carbonate

climate change A long-term change in the temperatures and weather patterns on Earth. Climate change often refers to global warming.

colonize The process by which a country takes control of another country or area by occupying it

commercial Relating to buying and selling goods

Commonwealth An association of 56 countries, most of which were once part of the British Empire

deposits An accumulation of a substance built up in the ground by a natural process

equator An imaginary line around the center of Earth, an equal distance between the North and South poles

estuaries Coastal areas where freshwater rivers and streams meet the ocean

ethnic Belonging to a group with a similar culture and background

export Sending goods to another country

faults Fractures or breaks in Earth's crust

fertile Capable of growing healthy plants

flax A plant whose stem has fibers used for textiles

freight Goods transported in large quantities by train, ship, plane, or truck

geothermal Energy that comes from heat within Earth

global warming The rise in Earth's temperature due to human activity

gourds Large fruits with hard shells

gradient A place where the ground slopes up or down

hospitality The act of being friendly and welcoming toward visitors

hydroelectric Relating to electricity produced from the power of flowing water

imported Brought in goods from other countries

inclusive Available for people of all abilities

independence Acting without the control or influence of others

infrastructure The systems and services that help a society operate, such as roads and power plants

ironsand A type of sand, dark gray or black in color, with a high amount of iron

irrigation The process of supplying water to crops

isthmus A narrow strip of land with sea on either side

methane A colorless and odorless gas that is the main component of natural gas

moderate Average or less extreme

molten Melted by high heat

multicultural Several different cultures in one group

nitrogen A colorless and odorless gas that makes up most of Earth's atmosphere

nutritional Having elements that provide nutrients, or nourishment for growth

ore Rock that contains valuable minerals

pesticides Chemicals that protect plants and crops from certain insects and animals

plantation An area where trees were planted for commercial purposes

pollinate To carry pollen to a plant so it can produce seeds

population density A measure of the number of people living per unit of land

precision Being careful, exact, and accurate

processed Treated or prepared in some way

productivity Efficient production of goods or services